EVERY LETTER TELLS A STORY: A RURAL POSTMAN'S TALE

By Martin Wigmore
Drawings by Megan Rose and Nanny

Copyright @ 2014 Martin Wigmore

978-1-291-71368-8

Inspired by the grandchildren and dedicated to family and friends who made it happen.

EVERY LETTER TELLS A STORY: A RURAL POSTMAN'S TALE

EARLY DAYS

First day dogs

In 1984 I started my new job as a part time postman - yes, in those days there was no talk of post-persons! The lady who was instructed to give me three days training was a hard, north-east lady called Mrs Coston. If you made a mistake in the prepping she would hit you with whatever she had in her hand or just her hand if nothing was available.

After a bruising first day I had got to know the other posties including William, Mrs Coston's son, who was working as a postman before going to uni to study history. But all I could see was his long hair! I had never seen a man with long hair down to his bottom before and when I'd seen him delivering I'd thought he was a woman! After my bruising three days training Mrs Coston still helped me, unpaid, for the rest of the week. She was really a kind lady inside if she liked you, but never cross her – or duck if you do.

My first day on my own was nearly my last as I had to deliver to a large house which backed onto the canal. I had been told to watch out for the two Alsatians. There was a high 10 foot fence all the way down to the house with the two large Alsatians barking at me from behind it. Feeling very safe with a fence between us I thought to myself I don't know why they bothered to warn me. As I approached the letter box it all went quiet so I posted the letters and turned around to walk back up the drive. To my horror there were two huge – yes this side of the fence they had become huge – very wet, very angry Alsatians which had jumped into the canal and swum round the back of the house to get to the drive I had to walk up. Fearing the worst and thinking 'I do not want to be a postie any more' the two

Alsatians came towards me. Just when I was preparing for the worst a little old lady no bigger than 4ft 6 inches opened the door and called them in with " Right boys you've had your fun, come on," and they trotted past looking at me as if to say, "She won't always be there to save you! "

So for the next few weeks it became a challenge to get to the letter-box unseen. I would tiptoe to the neighbour's house then with the letters in my mouth, both hands on the handlebars and my bottom in the air ride hell-for-leather down the drive hoping the Alsatians had not heard me, run to the door, push the letters through and dash away.

More hazards
Dogs were not the only things to be wary of. One bright sunny morning I was delivering to the Fox Caravan Park, a site on which the front doors of the caravans faced each other so the first caravan you came to you had your back to the front door of the caravan opposite. On this lovely warm sunny morning a beautiful long haired cat strolled by. I don't know why – perhaps perhaps I had been watching 'From Russia With Love' the night before – but I said "Good morning pussy-cat" in a very bad Russian accent. To my horror a voice replied "Good morning tiger" in a slow drawl. There was a lady at her front door having a fag! Very flustered I tried to explain "Sorry I was talking to your pussy." She burst out laughing, her cigarette went flying and a very embarrassed red-faced postman went on his way.

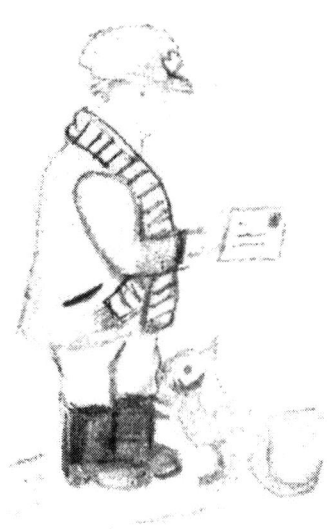

A little girl I had been speaking to on her way to play-school was starting big school for the first time. She looked very worried so I tried to cheer her up by saying, "What a lovely woollen hat you have on." She insisted I try it on and not wanting to upset her I pulled it on my head. She then said "Mummy says I must wear it as I have head lice." It quickly came off and I made a trip to the chemist on the way home making a mental note that I must think before speaking in future!

Full-time postie
My chance of a full-time post came round when William passed his exams and headed off to York University to pursue a Master's in History – which he achieved with flying colours – I found out many years later. He went on to teach at a university himself. Well done William!

To become a full time postie you had to pass a 1hour 45 minutes aptitude test and then an interview. Now it's 30 minutes on-line, so anyone can take it for you. How times have changed. At Leicester Head Office my friend Stuart Billing, a fellow postie who I already knew from school, went with me. But he only just made it as he had had a record 56 recorded deliveries on his second delivery round that day, as the Transport Minister had replied to all the complaints about the by-pass going through Proctor's Park. Those 56 were just 1 day's replies; there were hundreds more over the next few weeks, but to no avail as the by-pass still went ahead.

The replacement for my walk – postmen have 'walks', milkmen have 'rounds' apparently – was Margaret Steadman, a lovely lady in her late 50's. She had worked all her life and cared for her ailing mother but if that was not bad enough she came to work with us. Now it was my turn to be the teacher. Should I train Mags (as she was soon to be known) as I had been trained? If she did something wrong should I hit her the way Mrs. Cotton had hit me? Mags may have been small but she looked like she could handle herself so 'No' was the answer!

In those days we had pigeon-holes. Each one was a street split into odds and evens and when you had sorted like this you had to re-sort into numerical order, i.e. 2 to 10 , 10 to 20 etc. On Mags' first day out we had to cycle up a steep hill. On the way back, so as not to embarrass her, I stopped to walk up with her but she just cycled by with a laugh and a chuckle shouting "Try to keep up Martin!"

The walk she had to do was only part-time but had not been tested for years and had undergone a lot of development. I didn't get finished till 2.30pm and I was 25 years old, so I feared Mags would not stick at the job. However, despite not finishing till after 4pm most days – and we worked 6 days a week in those days – she stayed, and was a valuable member of staff and a good friend.

One day when we were short staffed she helped me do the farms in the car. To save time, I would drop her off and go on to the next bit and we'd meet up again. As I pulled onto the verge to make sure buses etc. could get by she opened the door, stepped out and disappeared out of sight! I had parked too close to the ditch and as she stepped out had landed straight into it. A few moments later I heard her cussing as she reappeared, like David Bellamy out of the jungle, with dried grass in her hair – but still the letters in her hands, bless her. She is now the church verger.

One day she was faced with a snarling dog and told us she had followed Post Office guidelines which are: If faced with a snarling dog show no fear and walk slowly away backwards. "So what happened Mags?" we asked. "IT BIT ME" was her reply. Back to the drawing-board, P O guidelines!

Long hours
My new full-time post was a split shift from 6 am till 1pm doing a delivery, then from 15.15 till 17.45 collecting letters from post-boxes in the van, and lastly visiting Post Offices for their final collections. They were very long hours! On a Saturday it was just the morning delivery – there were no afternoon collections.

The Post Office at Walton was owned by Mary Norvell – the mother of Duncan Norvell, the camp comedian. She was a lovely lady who spent many summer afternoons in the garden but was always on hand in case a customer did call in. Mary knew everyone in the village and even provided a tuck-shop for the children at no profit to herself. I never heard her say a bad thing about anyone in the village and she was a very good friend to me when my wife took seriously ill. Taking my wife to hospital was difficult. I had to use my allotted holidays as days-off to take her there. We could never book a time as I had to work in the morning and again in the afternoon, and in those days there were no appointments at weekends.

I think now would be a good time to explain how I asked my wife to go out with me. I first asked Dee "What would it take for you to go out with me? " She replied "Chloroform!" Not a good start, but undeterred I tried again a week later. I asked "What's Brazil famous for?" hoping she would reply "Coffee" and I could use the old chat- up line "Your place or mine?" but she replied "Nuts". I was speechless. But somehow we got together and 30 years later are still together with four children, six grandchildren and still laughing.

Mrs Tipping
My first postmistress was Mrs. Dorothy Tipping. It was not a good time to work for her as she had just lost her husband who had been the owner and postmaster. Mrs. Tipping had previously run a fashion shop in Loughborough and one in Barrow, but was not used to running a Post Office with its staff of postmen and women. And anyone who has just lost a loved one will know it's a very difficult time.

But Mrs. Tipping – I still call her that after knowing her for thirty years – was lucky in one respect in that she had Mary Brown to help her. Mary had been Mr. Tipping's assistant for a number of years and was very good on the counter. She helped a lot with Holy Trinity Church even, being part of the bell-ringing team. I used to joke that I would join the bell-ringing team if she would 'show me the ropes' but I think after the third time I said this it lost its 'a peal'. Yes, OK another bad joke!

Jessie Holland was also a very good long-standing friend of Mrs. Tipping. It was she who had got me my first part-time position as a postman. She had baby-sat Michael, the Tippings' son, who years later also worked as a postman for a short time. Mrs. Tipping was a smart business woman who I thought was very posh, so I was very surprised when she told me of the time she was delivering the mail to the farms on her bike and needed to answer a call of nature. The only option she had was to go behind a hedge into a field, but to her dismay just then round the corner came a local farmer called Arthur Kimber. "Do you need a dock leaf?" he shouted to Mrs. Tipping's dismay. At least she can laugh about it now.

A tragedy
The first few years brought plenty of smiles and a few tears. One sad event happened when I was delivering to the retirement home on North St and a young lad of about eleven came out and asked me to help his Nanna who, he said, had fallen out of bed. He ushered me towards a door and said "She's in there." I turned to ask him if she was decent and expecting someone to walk in but he had gone. So I knocked on the door and shouted "Are you OK? Do you need any help?" No reply so I knocked again and as there was still no reply I gingerly opened the door. The poor lady had died while trying to phone for help and had fallen into a cabinet with her head in an open space in the cabinet. I could not let her family find her like that as it was upsetting; it must have been why the young lad had run away.

I lifted her back onto the bed and covered her up the best way I could to give her some dignity. I put the phone back onto the receiver and was just about to go to her neighbour's and ask for her family's contact details when her daughter turned up. She was very upset, as you would expect, so I gave her a hug but didn't let her know how I had found her mother. I stressed that she must get a doctor to the bungalow so that the correct procedures could be followed, although I knew it wasn't easy to do when you have just found out your mother has died and your tears are flowing. I still had to complete my walk but I did it with a very heavy heart feeling sad for the family. They very kindly sent me a card thanking me for my kindness on that day.

CRIME

A Serious Post Office Robbery

My first ever experience of a serious Post Office robbery happened when I had been working at the PO for about two years. Mrs. Tipping had moved away from the flat above because living and working at the PO had become too much and she needed a change. The High St was closed to traffic while bridge repairs were taking place and you must remember that this was a time before everyone had a mobile phone. You had to rely on landlines to make phone calls.

The gang struck on a Monday night, breaking in through the back after putting foam into the alarm box high on the front wall, and lifting the telephone man-hole cover to cut off all the High St. telephones. (I can tell you all this now because the security system is completely different these days.) Once inside they then started to remove the internal counter, but this is when they must have been disturbed – or so we thought when we arrived for work at 5.30am and there were police everywhere.

However, the post must still go out so we had to try to work alongside the police and continue as best we could. It took about a day and a half to repair the phones and alarms but to everyone's amazement the gang struck again on the Thursday night of the same week! This time there was no messing about lifting man-hole covers to cut off the phones, as they simply used an axe to cut all the phone-lines off the pole. They removed the internal counters and poured oil on the floor to make it easier for them to move the safe to a stolen car. The people across the road were watching all this happen from their bedroom windows; the gang just waved at them and got the safe into the car boot but as they drove away it fell into the road. It was still there at 5.30am on the Friday morning, surrounded by police. According to the police the gang was from Sheffield. We never heard anything further and don't know if any of them were caught.

The Thief

In all the years I've worked for the Royal Mail I have only encountered one thief who worked as a postman, and it was thanks to my customers that he was caught so quickly.

One day as I was delivering on Thirlmere Road a lady came out and asked about a missing item. This is not strange on its own as packets do at times go missing because of wrong addresses, wrong post-codes or being delivered wrongly, but they nearly always turn up. I explained this and went on my way only to be stopped soon afterwards by a lady asking about missing birthday cards. (Birthday cards always bring back bad memories as when I first started on the post one lady had a lot of cards, so I stood at her door singing 'Happy Birthday To You'. Only when I had finished and she'd thanked me did she tell me that her husband had just died and they were bereavement cards.) But back to the thief story. Once the two people had grown to seven complaining about missing items I knew that it was too many to be an accident, so sought advice from my boss the Postmaster. I won't write his reply as it was not helpful or polite. I then asked my colleagues if they had been asked about missing items but they had not.

We had a new member of staff who was working as 'holiday cover'. He had been with us for about twelve weeks and at first had been very quick at sorting the mail but now was always the last out. He had been on my walk the week before all the complaints so I was very suspicious, but you can't just accuse someone. As the weeks went on more things went missing. I talked to Stuart and he said he thought he knew how he was selecting the cards with the money in and leaving the others. He then showed me, so now I knew what to look for too.

The culprit was definitely getting greedy but there was no point in talking to the Postmaster as he had been so rude to me earlier, so I phoned the manager and said I was 100% certain the new postman was stealing. I was then put in contact with the Internal Investigating Branch (I.I.B) who had to come to my house to take a statement. (This was so they had someone to blame in case I was wrong!) I explained what I knew and they agreed it sounded suspicious. They asked me to find people in the village who would be happy to receive cards containing notes which had had the serial numbers written down. I have some wonderful people on my round and I thought it only right the people who had been stolen from could see we were trying to catch the culprit, so asked them to help.

The day came when the I.I.B asked me to put the cards with the money into the sorting. I asked Mick, who was giving the suspect a lift to work, if he could be a little bit late so I had time to put the marked cards in. The I.I.B had drafted in others from Nottinghamshire as the suspect was a big lad, so if need be he could be quickly subdued. We kept in contact by mobile phone and they followed at a distance. After he had delivered to one street he went into a newsagents to buy fags. As he left, an I.I.B man asked the shop assistant to look at the money he had paid with, and sure enough it was money stolen from one of the cards. In hot pursuit they arrested him without any trouble and later searched his house where they discovered the full extent of his stealing, which included video games as well as money. When he went to court he received a community service sentence and was last seen working in a pub!

Chris and a contract- killing

For a few months my own son Chris also worked as a part-time postman after he left school, until he decided to return to full-time education. One of the reasons for his return to studying may have been because he was finger-printed in connection with a contract-killing. (His Auntie Gan will not be surprised to read this as she has always felt there was something strange about him and has openly admitted she would cross the road if he came walking towards her – which is probably why she lives in Hampshire.) The person killed was a night-club owner who lived in Barrow on the walk Chris was doing. The night-club was in Nottingham and police believe someone was paid to kill him. He was shot late one night in his driveway by someone who had made his own bullet. Despite the killing being re-enacted on Crime Watch – and it was on the programme again ten years later – nobody has ever been charged. Even a large reward for information was offered, but to no avail.

FRIENDS AND COLLEAGUES

Don Middleton the postman

When Don started at Barrow we had cardboard boxes on the front of the bikes instead of the pouches or bags. You could get more mail in them instead of coming back all the time, so you could do your delivery quicker. That box was not big or strong enough for Don; he used to use one of those plastic bread baskets.

Don, not being very tall but very strong, would pile it up high and could hardly see over the top. People waiting at bus stops would see a mountain of mail being pushed towards them and hear some cursing. Don was very good at cursing. One day a lady told me her husband was in bed and Don was trying to deliver a very awkward computer magazine. Her husband had served in the war and had never heard language like it. One day somebody had put a laughing-box, a joke-toy which laughs when you shake it, in the bottom of his basket. Every time he went over a bump it started laughing. At first he had no idea where it was coming from and it was very embarrassing as he passed the bus queue and all you could hear was laughing coming from Don's basket. He used to bring bunghole and beetroot sandwiches for Katie, a vegetarian post-lady who worked in our office. (Bunghole is cheese.) Don was always whistling and when I had the good fortune to work with his daughter I asked her if he whistled at home. She replied "He even whistles in his sleep."

Because you are out on your walk for long hours you sometimes need to wee. Don's friend had told him if he ever needs to go, he can go up the jitty behind his house. Unlucky for Don he miscounted the houses and was weeing up the neighbour's by mistake. They could not understand why in the hottest summer in years their fence was always wet until one day their son was playing in the garden, heard a noise, looked over the fence and was greeted with "What you looking at?"

After the early years of much change we began to get a settled work force together. Don Middleton transferred over from the Loughborough Delivery Office. He had been born and still lived in Barrow so it was a lot better for him as – apart from his National Service – he'd spent most of his life here.

For his National Service he had been posted to Cyprus. When I asked him if he had learnt any of the Greek language he said, " Yes. Jig-jig-Johnny-five-bob." That's Don for you. Other stories he told of his army days included one about driving to an RAF base in time for dinner. (Don never refused food. I have never seen anybody eat like him but he never put on any weight.) So off he went for his grub. The only trouble was later he forgot where he had parked his khaki-coloured truck. In among all the blue RAF ones you would think it would be easy to spot but no, it took him hours. And while cleaning his rifle one day food was called so off he went leaving his rifle leaning against a tree – until the sargeant brought it into the mess hall.

Don spoke his own language which we nicknamed 'Barrownese'; shoes were called kevs, trousers were clouts and you don't want to know what the old rivet was! I thought 'bing gone yonks' was an old Chinese friend of his but apparently it means having been away for a long time! One day he mended his bike and went for a test ride. As he got home he put the brakes on, went over the handle-bars but still landed on his feet to a round of applause from his neighbours. Don was great to work with; always a smile and a joke and a tale of good times.

Stuart Riley
Stuart Riley started at Barrow Post Office almost straight from school about twenty five years ago, and has been a great asset and a good friend ever since. He even came

into work, when officially on holiday, to cover my walk when my wife was rushed into hospital with a suspected heart attack.

Stuart is the joker in the office and some of the stories I am about to retell concern our old friend Don Middleton but please don't think Stuart's picking on Don. Don has been Stuart's dad's best friend since they were at school together, so Stuart has known Don all his life.

One day Mrs. Tipping, our first post mistress, was having a clear-out of old clothes and on top of the bag was a black bra. Stuart, whose quick mind was always on the lookout for a joke, thought if I put the bra in Don's coat pocket when he gets hot and needs to mop his brow, or when he wants to blow his nose, he will put his hand in his pocket and be surprised and amused to find a bra. Just a bit of harmless fun! But what happened was that Don didn't need to put his hand in his pocket and the bra stayed there. However, a little time later his wife was doing a crossword and needed a new pen. She asked Don if he had one and he replied that there was one in his coat pocket. You can guess what happened next and it wasn't the crossword that was finished!

Stuart must have had too much time on his hands on this occasion as he decided to loop together a lot of elastic bands – the ones used for bundling mail into streets. Poor Don, thinking he was pulling out one elastic band, began to pull out dozens all linked together, making him look like Paul Daniels doing the flower trick where he pulls out one and reams of flowers follow!

Stuart can also laugh at himself. One day he carefully wrote on his hands the numbers of the houses he had packets for then proceeded to put his gloves on so could not see what he had written!

Over the years we have laughed about something nearly every day, which takes some doing, but being a post man/woman you must have a sense of humour.

Nick Lewin
Nick joined us about twenty three years ago. Others had tried but failed to get to grips with the walk Nick has now made his own but Nick is a brilliant worker, quite outstanding and very trustworthy. He has a great sense of humour too and is a very good friend.

One day when he was quite new to the job he was delivering on Mill Lane in Barrow when a large dog came running down the road towards him. Nick took to his heels, ran to the safety of his bike and got it between himself and the dog. To Nick's relief, and the amusement of some young ladies who were at the nearby playground with their young children, the dog ran straight past still barking and running!

Nick now uses a high capacity trolley so that he can take all his packets and letters out at once and thus avoid coming back to the office. This is very good in normal, dry conditions but in snow and ice the trolley soon develops a mind of its own, seeming determined to make a break for freedom down the steep drives and roads of Nick's walk. In 2012 we had a very snowy winter and Nick could often be seen in hot pursuit of his runaway trolley looking like the brake-man from the team GB bob-sleigh team.

After a long week's work – we used to work six days a week when we started – the young Nick used to look forward to Saturday nights out with his mates. This particular Saturday night it was arranged that they would go to The Durham Ox, a nightclub where a 70's evening was advertised. The pub was on a duel carriageway towards Melton, a long way from where they lived, so they decided to go by mini-cab and be picked up for the return at 1.30am. Nick had assumed it was the music of the era only to his great disappointment it turned out to be the average age of the women! But all was not lost as he could have a good night with his mates until eleven – sadly no longer as the pub had forgotten to ask for a bar extension; and as the mini-cab was fully booked up to 1.30 it could not come to collect them any earlier. Well, I think we have all been there at some time or another. The only option was a long walk home; not the best night out.

Nick would love to get on the property ladder but on a postman's earnings it takes a long time, so he was quite taken with an advertisement for a house for only £7,000. It followed the success of the film 'The Lord of the Rings' and this was a Hobbit House. It was made of wood by a well known shed manufacturer, slept four and had a pull-out dining table in the living room. The only trouble is that Nick is six foot plus and the thought of him living in one of these reminded me of the classic film in which a six foot elf helps Santa, with very funny results.

Linda Conway
Linda has twice worked as a post-person. I remember asking myself when she first started, 'Why does she want to work? She has five kids under twelve and she would be better off claiming benefits.' The Post Office is great if you like working outside and meeting people but is not the best paid job in the world. So I just had to ask. Linda to her credit replied "I don't want to claim I just want to work." It turned out she also did cleaning at the bank and some nights at the petrol station! She's a one-woman work team. Linda's husband was training to be a teacher so could look after the children in the morning before school and there was always Linda's mum to help out as needed.

One story Linda told me went back to when she was eight months pregnant with her first

child. They didn't have a car to get to hospital in those days so her Mum took Linda on her
scooter. Linda is about twelve inches taller than her Mum and the scooter was only 50cc so the
sight of her going through Leicester on the back of this scooter and having to get off when it had to
go up a hill – at eight months pregnant – was funny, but to my mind also showed Linda's
very determined character.

That was just a little insight into what kind of person Linda is, so you won't be too surprised at
her determination to do the right thing in other situations that cropped up during her time at the Post Office. Linda's walk consisted of Cotes Rd and its outlying farms which she had to cycle round. It was very nice in the summer but horrible in bad weather. Some of the older farmers were a little strange to say the least. Linda talked to everyone, having known some of the farmers
since she was a little girl. Her Mum and Dad were well known in the village, which was much smaller then, so everybody knew everybody. One incident that springs to mind concerns a
couple called Mr and Mrs Martin. They had a strange marriage, often arguing and some days not
talking to each; both were very stubborn.

One day Linda asked Mr. Martin how Mrs Martin was only to be told she had died the week
before. Linda's response was to remark that it had been very sudden. His reply was "Yes, I just
thought she was not talking to me again." But it seems she had been dead in her chair for
two days before he realised anything was wrong.

One of the bleakest times was during the foot and mouth outbreak. The farmers on Linda's walk were not just customers but had become friends, so to see the news every night with pictures of devastated farmers having their animals destroyed made Linda wonder if it could happen to her friends. One morning, when delivering to the smallholding of an Italian man who had spent all his life in the Merchant Navy, saving up to buy this tiny farm on which to live with his wife and children, she was aware as she got to the door that there were no animals, no birds, just an uneasy quiet. She feared the worst. All of a sudden he appeared behind her, his hands dripping with blood and a big knife in one hand that immediately caught the eye. He said in broken English "The chicken no longer lays any eggs." Then he held up a dead chicken in the other hand. Linda gulped a deep breath of relief and hastily made an exit!

We meet all sorts on the post. Most people are wonderful but like everywhere in life there are always exceptions. Linda was delivering to the caravan site on North St one day when she had to knock on a door to deliver a packet. As the man opened the door his dressing gown came open exposing his privates. Thinking it was just an accident and could happen to anyone she continued on her walk, but as this happened four times in the next two weeks it became apparent it was no accident.

After a chat with the wife of the site-owner it was thought the best option was to inform the police, because it could be a paper-girl next time. It wasn't nice having to give a statement about what had happened but if good people do nothing the devil wins. Then the long drawn out legal process started. There were hearings cancelled or wasted and a lot of time spent in court. The whole process took nearly two years but to Linda's credit she did not waver, thinking that if it prevents someone else from having to go through all this it will have been worth it.

It turned out the man was already known to the police for under-aged sex with two young girls and Linda, who had to give evidence to the court against a defence barrister trying to save his client, was successful and the man found guilty. But alas the sentence seemed too little after such a long struggle for justice. Sometimes it's not enough just to be a post-person; you also have to do the right thing.

I feel I would be amiss not to tell you that Linda had been diagnosed with breast cancer and during the court hearings had gone through the trauma of diagnosis, an operation and chemotherapy which at times did bring her very down. But it never prevented her from doing the right thing so that other people would be safe. I would like to think I would have done the same; but you can never be sure until you are in the same situation.

One amusing thing did happen to her while she was being driven home from hospital almost at the end of her chemotherapy treatment. You need to remember that Linda had lost all her hair and eyebrows at the time, but on seeing a young man on his bicycle hit the kerb and fall off into the road she was straight out of the car and rushed over to help. But the poor man took one look at this hairless woman striding towards him that he jumped to his feet, dragged his bike up and fled, looking over his shoulder from time to time in disbelief, probably thinking 'I must have banged my head - this is not real.' At least Linda could see the funny side!!

John Kimber

John Kimber joined our happy unit about 1998. At first he only did a part-time 'Walk' so he could carry on building up his construction business, but unfortunately due to people not paying for work done – and him having to pay for materials and such – he ended up working for the Royal Mail full time. It's strange how circumstances shape our lives. I go trout fishing with John and we always have a good laugh even if we don't catch anything, which always brings amusement and ribbing from the others in the office. And to fish you need equipment.

John is very tight with money and I must say I begrudgingly admire his attitude because I find it very hard to say 'No', but John went to the same tackle-shop for five years looking at a £7 landing-net before finally buying it! John drives the van and delivers to the factories and out-lying farms and the village of Seagrave. John is not the tallest of people, just over 5ft 5inches, and Royal Mail had decided to change its policy on wearing shorts. For many years shorts were banned from being worn as deemed unfitting and not smart enough, but they changed policy and said they could be worn. With this change also came a change in colour from royal blue to a red T-shirt for summer. Unfortunately, it was exactly the same colour as Seagrave Primary School's T shirt. John always seemed to get there about break time (we think Tuck Shop time) and as he was leaving one day after having delivered the mail a teacher shouted at him "You boy! Where do you think you're going ?" They both had a shock when John's grizzled face turned round. To make it worse he came back and told us!!

John is responsible for one of the Post Office's funniest incidents. I always try and book a week's holiday in late October to go to Bradgate Park to watch and listen to the deer and enjoy the changing trees. It's a lovely time of year. When I explained this to John, while we were sorting one day, John chirped up with "You know what Bradgate is famous for?" Slight pause. " Dogging." Without hesitation Debbie piped up "I was addicted to that. I used to go out every night after work and twice at weekends." We all just looked at her in silence until Nick said "That's illegal." Debbie said "Oh no it's not. I used to go out with a policeman who did it." We were all in stitches at her honesty and the way she carried on talking about how great it was on a summer's evening and the virtues of being outside. It was not until John said " You *are* talking about dogging, aren't you?" that she said "No, I thought you said JOGGING!!"

Sharon Newman
Sharon joined our happy little band of hard working posties about six years ago and I was lucky enough to be asked to train her. I must confess she was head and shoulders above everybody else I had previously trained because you only had to tell her something once. You never had to repeat yourself.

The only thing that worried me was when she had to ride the bike. Any parent will know how it feels when you have to watch your child ride their bike for the first time without stabilizers and you have to watch them wobble down the road fearing any moment it will end in a fall. I did explain that pavements were for pedestrians but that seemed to fall on deaf ears, so I was very sorry for anyone unfortunate enough to get in her way.

Sharon is called Wincey by her friends in the office after a weather girl who used to be on ITV. This is because it is very important in the unpredictable British weather to have some idea if it's going to rain, hail or snow when out on duty. Sharon spends lots of time watching and listening to weather reports. She also has two weather apps on her phone and I don't mind admitting she is very good even when pushed to give the approximate time of the rain's arrival during the day. The only thing I'm doubtful about is when she tells me she can smell when it's going to snow. However, if at any time you feel like travelling and are worried about snow just ask me and I'll phone her and ask her to put her nose out of the window. I'll let you know.

Sharon has a really good sense of humour and does not mind sharing her mishaps with us, bless her.   One funny moment came whilst delivering mail in Seagrave, Sharon having got there in the van. The poor woman had to go through two gates to reach the letter box but unfortunately the gardener's Rottweiler was loose in the garden and kept preventing her from getting back to the van. Every time the dog wandered off and Sharon thought she was safe, as soon as her hand went on the gate it was back barking. Poor Sharon was reduced to shouting for help. After about twenty minutes a group of ramblers appeared and heard her calls for help. Not fearing for their own safety, they lured the dog away so that finally Sharon could make her escape shouting thank you as she drove away.

But alas that was not the end of the story. One of our stand-in postman from Rearsby, Mick Thompson was his name, arrived at work one morning with a cheeky grin and carrying their local news pamphlet 'The Rearsby Scene'. In 'The Ramblers' news-piece it stated that 'While enjoying a spot of blackberry picking in Seagrave there could be heard a damsel post-lady in distress who needed rescuing.' Poor Sharon; weeks later the event had come back to haunt her.

Funny, strange events, seem to happen to Sharon. Once whilst delivering on Sileby Rd. a poor motor cyclist was struck in the face by a pigeon which knocked him off his bike and left him feeling dazed. Until the paramedics came, Sharon stayed with him and made sure he was OK. On another occasion whilst doing Stuart's walk with the trolley she managed to lose a wheel. Stu has been using that trolley for years with no mishaps; Sharon had it for one day and loses a wheel. What's more she couldn't find where it went even with the people of Melton Road helping her!

Sharon recently went into a block of flats but unfortunately whilst upstairs a door became stuck and refused to open. Being two floors up and stranded, with no response to her calls for help, she decided to phone me. After listening to her story, having a chuckle to myself and quickly finding my camera and note book, I set off thinking 'I'm glad it's not me.' However, her own brute force opened the door before I could get there.

Sharon is a great person to work with, always ready to help, and very efficient at her job. But she doesn't just work, she has other responsibilities too, as she is the mother of two fine girls who are a great advertisement for her own and husband Toby's parenting skills. Her caring side came out once again in Seagrove when a lady asked her to stay and wait while the ambulance came to pick up her dying husband. In this job you never quite know what you are going to face but Sharon has never been found wanting even in some very trying circumstances.

Geordie Mik

Geordie Mik - that's not a spelling mistake, that's how he signs his name! Mik joined us about ten years ago, and like many of us who started on the post, it was just until something better came along and better than being unemployed. As his name suggests he is from Newcastle, the love of his life, after his wife Karen and the children Harley and Bailey.

As a youngster he had a trial for Newcastle United and played in a band called 'Revolution'. There is a picture of the band in the office and you have to guess which one he is. Most people get it wrong. When he first left school he worked in a shipyard joining pieces of metal together. (Sounds very riveting – sorry, could not resist!) It just shows what varied backgrounds we all come from; his knowledge of music is amazing. And he's a keen runner too. He did many Great North Runs for charity. Unfortunately he needed both hips replacing this year and so has been out of action for most of it.

Being a part-time postman was not enough to pay all the bills so to his credit he also has a night time job. These Geordies are not afraid of hard work. Mik has done all the Walks in the village at some time or other so if a letter arrives with just the name of the person on but no address he is the first one we ask. To our amazement quite often he knows. Geordie Mik, whose real name is Mik Richardson, has been a real asset to the team .

INCLEMENT WEATHER

Being a post person for nearly thirty years I have endured all sorts of conditions from terrible blizzards to summer heat waves. The blizzards are sometimes so bad that the snow hits you full in the face and clogs up the wheels of your bike so making it very hard to push. Summer heat-waves are days when everyone tells you it's a great day to be a post person! They don't seem to realise you're out in it for hours and it's hard to keep hydrated when there's no public conveniences in the village and a call of nature means a long ride back to the post office. So many people have cameras on their properties these days even a quiet corner is out of the question unless you want to end up on YouTube!

Snow and ice seems to bring out some of the funniest moments. While I was delivering on Sileby Road one day I saw an elderly lady fall on the ice at a bus stop so I went over to help her up and make sure she was OK; but as I walked away from her I fell over, so she then came over to help me up! What passing motorists thought I'll never know.

When I first started on the Royal Mail people would clear

their paths to their doors as a priority and still today some of the older generation do; but unfortunately the new 'claim-all-you-can-society' means that if someone falls on your path and you have tried to clear it you could be responsible for damages. I think it's a very big shame and should be the other way round. Post office van drivers have other problems in snowy icy conditions such as badly parked cars and children on sledges; they are certainly no respecters of the Highway Code sledging down snowy roads when the schools are closed.

I must admit the standard of snow men has improved a great deal over the years. When I first started it was two balls of snow one on top of the other, a carrot for the nose and two pieces of coal for the eyes. Now I have witnessed snow penguins, and snow women dressed in dresses; one just had a bra and pants. (How do you tell a snow man from a snow woman? Yes, you're right. Snowballs! It may be old but so am I.) One snowman, made by the Toon family on Ennerdale Road, was easy to spot as a snow*man* as I've never seen a carrot placed *there* before!!!!!!!

Rain. Some days the rain just seems to wait until you leave the office and finish when you do. The Royal Mail provides you with waterproofs and Wellingtons if you have to deliver to a farm or building site, and they are needed. One day Nick was busy tucking his waterproofs into his Wellingtons until it was pointed out his Wellingtons would fill with water. The things we do when tired!! Keeping the mail dry on rainy days is a very big challenge. You do your best but even if the mail is dry when taken from your pouch, by the time you get to the door the water has soaked from your wet hands and is being absorbed by the paper. It may seem to the householder you have not tried at all, which is very frustrating.

High winds can play havoc with your delivery, blowing your bike over, and if you're really unlucky the elastic bands can break leaving you chasing letters down the street. I think we have all experienced that at some time. Some days, in the great span of British Weather, we have had all four seasons in one day – snow, rain, hail and sunshine. On one occasion, which I did only experience once in thirty years, it was raining on one side of the street – North Street in Barrow – and not the other.

Due to changes in our start times we are out later in the day, and on a personal note I do not like delivering in hot weather. When it's cold you can put more on but when you are too hot there is only so much you can take off. One very kind lady pulled up in a car one day with a bottle of flavoured water saying " No one goes thirsty on my watch", and I have some wonderful people who ask if I need a drink, but as I explained earlier, what goes in must come out. Sun block is very important too; just remember to rub it in, otherwise young children can mistake you for having ice cream all over your face.

WEIRD AND WONDERFUL PO STAFF

In those early years we seemed to have a very large turn-over of staff as many new employees stayed for very short periods – in some cases for just a few hours, others only a couple of days. I remember one chap saying, after we had done the prepping- up (sorting the letters and packets into the delivery order), "What's next?" I said "We now take them out." He said "Not likely", got his coat and left, never to be seen again. It did give you a chance to meet many weird and wonderful people who seemed to see life in a different way.

One lady, who came on a scooter, did not like to turn right while driving it. She would turn left at the roundabout near the office, drive along a bit, then stop, get off and walk the scooter across the road so she could turn left at the roundabout. It made coming to work a long journey. She arrived at work one day with a moisturising cream on her cheeks, nose and forehead. That's not strange you may think but she had not rubbed it in. It was like working with someone on manoeuvres in the army. Not wishing to upset her, nobody said anything hoping she would notice herself. But in the end I had to say "Sorry, but you can't go out on delivery like that" as she was heading out the door.

Two men, who were friends, came to work at our office at the same time. The strange thing about these men was that as you tried to explain about the sorting you did not get back the usual questions. I would say "Did you understand that?" and they would ask "Is that safe alarmed or bolted to the floor?" They left after three days and the Post Office got broken into three weeks later. Maybe coincidence or not but they didn't get away with anything. Not this time anyway.

Sunderland Sean was a nice lad who worked with us for a short time and will be remembered for how he drove back from Loughborough with fence panels bungie-strapped to the roof of his car, only to discover that he had lost one of them by the time he got home and the other was only fit for firewood.

Debbie Terry worked with us for two years and the room was never quiet with Debbie about. She had travelled across Russia by train on her own, and been to the Far East with a charity group, as well as visiting many other countries – but I will always remember her for two reasons. The first was seeing her trying to fish her mobile phone out of a drain. The second for starting a sentence with "To cut a long story short" and still be talking twenty minutes later without taking a breath until I said "And this is the short version."

Katie Deadmam used to cycle from West Leake every day – a round trip of about 20 miles – even in the winter. She had a great sense of humour and was well liked by all the staff.

POSTMASTER OR MISTRESS – AN IMPORTANT ROLE

When I first started, all those years ago, the postmaster or mistress had a very important role which was well respected and well paid. All the old age pensions were paid over the counter and on Thursday mornings the queue would stretch along Barrow High Street. There was no pushing-in and people would queue for as long as thirty minutes before opening time.

One day, in my first year, a man collapsed in the queue and a doctor was called from the local surgery. He pronounced him 'Dead at the scene' so he was moved into the back awaiting collection, but the counter staff carried on serving, not out of a lack of respect but because the queue was getting too long.

The only time I can remember the Post Office being closed, apart from the aftermath of break-ins, was before Barrow High St was redesigned. It couldn't happen now but then a car lost control and crashed through the shop door and window. This was well before drive-ins became popular for fast food! That afternoon, Mrs Tipping and Mary Thompson had a well-earned rest after their surprise visitor.

Over the years different governments have reduced the need to go to a post office because you can now carry out nearly all the transactions on-line. The sad fact is the poor postmaster or mistress now has to try to sell other products to make ends meet, so please don't get upset if you are asked if you want insurance etc. They're only trying to make a living for their families.

During the last few years robberies have changed. In earlier years break- ins happened during the night, when the office was closed and so no one was injured. Unfortunately, over the last few years people have been put at risk by daylight robberies. Tony, a Barrow postmaster, had the door broken down as he was trying to lock up and a knife held to his throat, whilst two other assailants robbed the safe and got away over the back. They left a very shaken postmaster who unfortunately, because he had not locked the safe first, had to replace the stolen money himself. This was the final straw and as soon as possible he sold the business and left.

The most appalling crime against a postmaster happened just last year in 2012 and to his great credit the man in question returned to the role when many would have sold up and moved on, especially as the rewards of running a post office are not great any more. But to explain in a little more detail. Last winter on a very snowy day Bob, the postmaster, had locked up the post office, returned to his car and was driving back to his home some fifteen miles away when his mobile rang. He pulled over to answer it and as the car stopped a man from the car behind him pulled up, opened Bob's door, forced Bob out at gun point and made him get into the back seat of the his own car. Bob's head was pushed down and he was threatened all the way back to the post office so it must have seemed ages travelling back in the dark into the unknown.

The abductors demanded the keys and codes to enter the post office and drove up the side drive which leads into the back of the post office. However, as luck would have it, some time earlier a policeman had been called to the High Street responding to reports of children throwing snowballs and causing trouble in general. To the policeman's great credit he thought it very strange for a car to be driving up there at that time and went to investigate. Very fortunately for Bob his two captors saw the policeman and ran away over the back gardens towards the railway lines, leaving the car behind; and Bob too, shaken but thankfully physically unharmed.

What the men would have done inside I don't know. The safe is on a time-lock and so well anchored to the floor there is nothing Bob could have done! The car that was left abandoned was full of forensic evidence and helped catch one of the men, together with television appeals and newspaper coverage. Bob had a few days off but in true post office tradition returned to work. After many months the man was sentenced to prison, where I hope he stays for a long time.

Not all postmasters had to deal with theft and robberies. Two very nice ladies, Sheila and Dashier, moved house to run the post office in Barrow after Dashier's husband died very suddenly. Dashier needed a change so the two sisters came and ran the post office most successfully. They were well liked. It was not easy but their father was on hand to help with maintenance when he was not fund-raising for a place of prayer in their Indian home land. Being Hindu meant we were introduced to new customs, beliefs and party food! It all went very well for about three years but unfortunately, due to family problems, once again it became time to sell up and move on. It was very sad.

Over the years many postmasters and mistresses have come and gone. I remember Mike and Rose. Rose was a teacher and I'm afraid living and sleeping over the sorting office did not go down well with her. We used to start at 5.45am in those days and unloading the mail from the van, sorting the boxes and bags, and the noise of early morning post office banter was not conducive to getting a good night's sleep. I fully understood when they too decided to sell the business

A FEW OTHERS I WOULD LIKE TO MENTION

There are a few others I would like to mention but will just use their first names and the initial of their surnames as I have not been in contact with them for a few years and so have not gained their permission to use their full names.

Mick K. was a great help to me and my wife as she'd had to have the same operation as Mick, so Mick gave us lots of advice and tips on how to cope with the great upheaval that was about to alter our lives. It was a great help to have someone who had been through it all and was willing to answer any questions you felt the doctors did not have the time to answer or feel worth answering.

One of Mick K's jobs was to drive the Seagrove van which in the afternoons I had to use to make the collections from post boxes and post offices. This particular day the usual van had broken down and the garage only had a security van to lend us. Mick had finished his duty and left. I did not start my duty till 15.15 so he had not had the opportunity to explain how to open the doors easily. There was a key to use from the outside but once you had got inside, adjusted the seat and closed the door, you realized there was no door handle and that the windows were welded shut for security reasons. So I sat there and spent the next twenty minutes looking for a way out! I was just about to drive round to his house and sit outside pipping the horn, when I noticed a small lever by my feet and fortunately that opened the door, so with great relief I was able to set off without having to embarrass myself any more.

Mick K. must, as far as I know, go down in post office history as the only person who filled in the accident book with 'Ostrich attack'. This happened as he was delivering to a farm on Black Lane. Farmers and their tenants sometimes don't have letter boxes on their front doors but make provision by having boxes put at the edge of their land where the postman can leave their letters, packets, etc. in a safe, dry place. On this occasion it was a box at the corner of a paddock where the farmer was trying to raise ostriches for meat. Mick was bending down, putting mail in the box when said ostrich took a liking to his ear!

Pete R

Pete was a manager at our parent office in Loughborough. He'd come to our little sub office to cover a Walk whenever someone was off unexpectedly, perhaps ill. That's the problem when you work in a small office as everyone has their 'Walk' and there is no one spare to fill in. Holidays have to be booked a year in advance so the Royal Mail know they have someone to cover that Walk. Over the years we have been asked to cover as many as three Walks in one day due to people being off sick. When I first started as a postman overtime was compulsory; no one went home until all the mail was delivered. Until four years before I started, mail was still delivered on Christmas Day! But back to Pete. We liked him coming as he could not believe we did not get the same delivery equipment as our parent office. Until he arrived we didn't even know we were entitled to a lot of helpful things such as a pair of Wellingtons if you had a farm on your delivery, special scissors to cut the bag-ties or the ability to use bulk-drops if you had a lot of mail, or small packets for the same address. We had been told you were only entitled to one pair of shoes a year and had to buy any more if they did not last. This wasn't true. Pete soon put all that right, bless him. Sadly he has now retired, but whenever I see him he still asks if we are getting all we are entitled to.

THE MOST IMPORTANT PEOPLE

In my opinion the most important people are the customers and I am very lucky to have some great people on my 'walk'. I am sorry I cannot mention them all but here are just a few stories I can share with you as I have asked permission.

Mr and Mrs Cunningham

Mr and Mrs Cunningham were both very successful teachers and thanks to Fred I can retell this story. One day Mrs Cunningham, a very good music teacher who has helped many of the village children, was delighted to see the house-sign 'Mozart' go up on a new neighbour's door. She thought that a like-minded neighbour, who loved their music, had just moved in. Soon she was delighted to have the chance to ask her neighbour, Mrs North, about the house-sign but the reply she got wasn't what she expected! The reason for the name was that Mrs. North's first name was Maureen (Mo) and her husband's Arthur, and if you cut them both short then put them together you get Mozart!

I asked Fred if he had any other stories and he recalled that one day, on a school trip, he and a fellow teacher had to get a class of school children over a swollen stream. One teacher had to stand in the water and another pass them over, which after a while was quite tiring. He remembers holding one child who suddenly asked "Anywhere round here I can buy a stamp? I would like to write to my mum."

Terry Brooks

Terry Brooks has had more than his fair share of heart-break and I don't mind admitting I had a tear in my eye when he told me this story about what should have been a very proud day. Terry, after forty years working as a chef at Loughborough University, was rewarded with a Queen's

Garden Party invitation for his long service. Unfortunately, his wife Sandra had been taken ill and was in hospital, but still very excited about going and was planning what to wear when she suddenly died just a few days before the Buckingham Palace Party. A wife's death is very distressing at any time but to his great credit he still decided to go, but with his wife's picture in his pocket. So she was still there with him to share in their lifetime's dedication. Thank you Terry for letting me share that.

Georgina Hartley
Mrs Hartley is a wonderful lady with a great sense of humour. I first met her about twenty years ago because I had to take a broken Christmas present to her. You could tell it was broken by the sound of glass in the box yet I was hoping I was mistaken and that it was a jigsaw. It should have been the van driver's job to take it but he refused, and I knew that before a broken item can be returned it has to be delivered first. I said I'd take it. Mrs Hartley was not amused with the broken contents and told me to stand just inside the door while she phoned the company to complain. Luckily for me the company quickly answered, told her to release me, and that they would send a replacement. Georgina is a very straight talking lady as many a door to door sales-person has found out. I doubt many have returned and some probably still have nightmares after meeting with Georgina.

One day, while delivering on the opposite side of the road, I could hear her calling to me. As I started to cross the road I could see a mist-like thing in front of her door. I stopped on the spot as I realised it was a swarm of very angry bees. Georgina told me to come inside but passing through a million bees did not appeal so I just stood a little nearer and tried to offer help and advice. I told her to ring the council and seek help from the Pest Control Department. If they could not help they would know who to contact. (I should mention Georgina is in her eighties.) I carried on my round while she made the phone calls and said I'd call back again at the end of my duty to make sure she was OK.

When I went back I learnt that Georgina had made the phone call to the council but was told they could not help. However they did give her the number of a bee keeper; unfortunately he did not answer. I could see that the bees had all gone except for a few stragglers and asked what had made them leave. I should not have been surprised by the reply but I was. It seems they had all swarmed around the queen and Donna, a great friend from across the road, had come across with a cardboard box and gathered them up. Then I asked where they were now. To my surprise she very sheepishly replied that they hadn't known what to do so had put them in the wheelie bin which had just been emptied! I must apologise to any refuse collectors injured on that collection day but after trying the proper authorities, and being left with no help, this was the only way Georgie could resolve the situation.

One bright sunny day Georgina was out in the garden when suddenly she felt a very sharp pain in the centre of her chest. Fearing the worst, thinking she was having a heart attack, she sat down only to discover that it wasn't her heart but a wasp. She'd been stung. Much to her delight the pain didn't seem so bad, so feeling relived and laughing to herself, she went to the post office to carry out some business. Here she was quite happily sharing her 'wasp-sting experience' with the post ladies, Shelia and Dashier, even opening her blouse to show them the point of the sting when she heard the shop door open. Without thinking she turned to see who was coming in still with her blouse open. The poor man turned and fled. He didn't know he had just experienced a 'Georgia' moment!

Nick and Amanda Elliot

Nick, a manager, and Amanda, a nurse, are two of the nicest people you could meet because they're always ready for a cheery word and a chat. But one day that changed! I'll explain why. The story starts when a nice old couple moved from London to Barrow to be near one of their daughters who, as it happened, worked in the same hospital as Amanda. The couple lived here for about eighteen months until sadly the husband died leaving poor Marge on her own. It must have been very lonely for Marge and she started looking out for company. Two people who often passed her house were Amanda and Nick as they frequently walked past with Basil, their long-haired golden retriever. He was a really special dog as he had a lovely temperament and was a delight to talk to.

Amanda, being a nurse, worked different shifts every week and so Nick would nip home to take Basil out if Amanda wasn't able to. As you can guess both became easy targets for poor Marge who would rush out to talk to them, yet I was even easier as I was pushing a bike and stopping at every house! Marge was a lovely lady but when you have people waiting for their mail you can't stand talking for long. After hearing about the blitz and how they used to go dancing in their dinner break during the war it was always nice to see Amanda or Nick walking with Basil as it gave me a chance to make my excuses and get away. This was not just a one-sided affair because it worked for them as well if they had been stopped first .

Unfortunately Marge got worse and would tell you something and then repeat it word for word just like a record. Please don't think I'm calling her; I'm just trying to explain the circumstances.
On one particular Saturday, Marge had held me up for about ten minutes. I had politely told her there were people waiting for their mail and then tried to walk away, but despite this she would grab hold of the handle bars and stop me. Then my eyes lit up as I thought salvation was at

hand; I saw Nick, Amanda and Basil come walking down the road. I could get away at last! But no! Amanda had seen Marge and she knew what would happen if they were seen. Much to Nick's amazement they came to a shuddering halt. Poor Basil! The halt was so sudden I thought he would be wearing a neck brace the next time I saw him. After only a very brief exchange of words Nick and Amanda did a U turn and disappeared back up the road along with my hopes of freedom. To my amazement only a few minutes later they returned in their car, all three smiling and waving as they sped by!

Mrs L

Mrs L came to our country after the 2nd World War from Eastern Europe. I'm not sure if it was Russia or the Ukraine as I didn't like to ask too many questions. As she is a lovely lady and I would hate to say the wrong thing, or give the wrong impression, I'll just call her Mrs. L. She is known to most of the village who went to the local school in the 60's, 70's and 80's because she was a dinner lady there for over thirty years. She certainly looked after my four children as if they were her own and I think most children liked her a lot. One of my sons, Chris, would always have his shoe laces undone and Mrs L would always make a point of telling him and helping him to do them up.

One day, while Chris was getting ready for school, his mum noticed his shoe was split and not having a spare pair, or time to buy any new shoes, she decided to super glue the split hoping it would last until the weekend when we could get another pair. This sounded like a good plan but unfortunately Chris had PE that day. Mrs L spotted him crossing the play ground with one plimsoll on and one shoe on and enquired why. I don't think she was expecting the reply "The shoe is super glued to my foot and won't come off".

THE CHANGES AHEAD

Like all businesses the Royal Mail needs to change with the times. Last year the Mail Centre in Leicester was closed and moved to Northampton and all post-persons were issued with a 'personal delivery assistant'. No, not a little person to run alongside you but a device to log 'Tracked' items and 'Signed For' items. These devices send instant reports back to a web-based data storage unit so that customers can check to see where their item is.

A lot of delivery offices have already lost their stock of bicycles. This is because deliveries in the future are likely to use van-sharing and high capacity trolleys; take photos of your posties with bikes now before they become things of the past!

Hopefully people will continue to use the Post Office and the Royal Mail and after my time post will still be delivered by post persons who are a part of the community and care about the community. One who springs to mind is David Martin, who despite being young really does care about being polite and making sure the customer is happy with the service. 'Going the extra mile' used to be the term used in the Royal Mail. He has a great sense of humour and even laughs at my jokes, so if we can find more like David I think the Royal Mail will be in safe hands.

MY PERSONAL THANKS

I would like to thank the residents of Barrow because over the years at some point or other I have delivered to all of the village and have always loved meeting new people. I have been lucky to share in people's joy when delivering good exam results and seeing the sheer joy on their faces as they shared their news, and again seeing people's faces light up when they get an unexpected letter from an old friend. I have also delivered love letters to couples and been able to witness it develop into marriage and children. A kind soul once said to me that post-people are the glue of society and I now understand exactly what was meant in that statement. I feel very fortunate that in my line of work I have met some wonderful people and although I have witnessed some very sad times I have been lucky enough to see the way friends rally round and the overwhelming kindness in people in times of trouble. I don't think you get that same feeling from receiving an email; the letter in the post seems so much more intimate. Somebody has written a letter and posted it and it's been hand-delivered. Sadly emails and texts seem to be taking over but I have loved every moment of being your postman. Thank you.

In memory of Troy Harrison, rural manager, who died aged 49 on the 22/01/2014. 'Fine and dandy'.

Printed in Great Britain
by Amazon